Fight Like a Grown Ass Woman

An Inspirational Interactive Healing Journal For Women Battling Breast Cancer

NEW EDITION

MARENDA TAYLOR

ISBN-13: 978-1727597110

Printed in the United States of America

Foreword

Put on your big girl panties and fight!!! Fight like your life depends on it, because it does!!!!

Good words to use as a mantra as you embark on this journey of the body, mind and soul.

You will be different after this journey...

I too had Cancer.
But it never had me... Not thru the surgeries, nor the challenging chemo regimen, not through the radiation treatments.

No, I had cancer; it never had me.
I woke up every day, forced a big smile, looked in the mirror and said to myself - "ok, self, let's do this!!"

Welcome to the "I had CANCER club," a club none of us wanted to join, but once here you have a question and a choice to make...

Will you let Cancer tear you down and rebuild yourself into the beautiful WARRIOR PRINCESS you are? Or, are you gonna let it take over all your waking hours with worry and doubt and fear?

MARENDA TAYLOR has captured the spirit of the fight in this beautiful book that gently guides you from a perspective of one who has been there and won the battle beautifully!!!!

Over the past 2 years I have watched Marenda as we both fought the fight and I must say from the bottom of my heart she has been and continues to be one of the biggest inspirations of my life, and that is saying a lot!!!

I wish you love and light and healing as you complete the following pages of this compassionately tailored book built for each and every woman who ever needs to be reminded to GET UP AND FIGHT LIKE A GROWN ASS WOMAN!!!!

Don't ever forget – YOU ARE WORTH IT!!!

Lynde Hartman –
Cancer Survivor and voice from the other side.

Reflections of a Survivor

No one prepared me for this sucker punch. How did I get so blindsided? It's like I was wearing a seat belt and still I got ejected. Not only was my world turned upside down and everything I knew to be true seemed questionable- including my part in this nightmare -but what the hell just happened?

At age 42 with two children a vibrant career and healthy lifestyle, I was diagnosed with breast cancer. Devastated and feeling betrayed by my body, my mind began to do the same.

My thoughts invaded my head like bees drawn to a hive. My sanity left me like the waves on a shore. Somewhere between pain and hope between God and me I knew had to choose. I had to choose to fight. And Fight Like A Grown Ass Woman.

Like so many of us I went through life holding on to so many painful memories and carrying my past traumas like a backpack on a hiking trail. I wore regrets and remorse like a uniform; putting it on everyday like it was my duty.

It wasn't until I gave myself the gift of self-reflection and mental maintenance that I began to peel away my layers of veils, so I could see how to heal myself with the divine love and guidance that was within me.

Allowing myself the space to hear and express the desires of my silenced soul gave a voice to my forgotten dreams and opened me up to a new world of possibilities. With each new insight I became a bit less heavy and began to spread my wings like a caged bird set free.

I recommend every woman use this journal to capture and connect to their deepest thoughts, hopes and dreams. Use it as a guide to design the life you know you know were destined to have and then *Fight Like A Grown Ass Woman* for it!

Myla Rahman -
Survivor & Thriver

You Are My Warrior

A Poem for Breast Cancer Survivors from Those Who Love You,
But Don't Know What to Say or What To Do.
By TC Cooper
President of UpwardAction®
Founder of CooperZone™ Academies

Your journey may feel lonely;
Know that you are not alone.

You may be scared;
Know that my prayers are with you.

I may annoy you because I say the wrong things or don't ask the right questions;
Forgive my actions, focus on my love.

I may disappoint you because I don't visit or call enough;
Know that I love you, but I don't know what to say or do to make it better.
It breaks my heart that I can't make it go away, so I may sit quiet and pray.

Know that I am always thinking about you,
Praying for you,
Sending you love,
Transmitting all of the healing energy and prayers that my body, spirit and soul can muster.

I see the dark side of your struggle,
the one you don't talk about or share on social media.

I see the pain from the needles,
and it breaks my heart.

I see the hurt from the poking and prodding, and
I may close my eyes, because
It's too painful to watch, and
Seeing you in pain reminds me of my inability to help.

I see your fatigue and moments of despair, and
I may not say anything about it because,

I love you so much, and,
I don't know what to say, and
my inability to make it better hurts to much.
Forgive me.

BUT
Know that as much as I see your hard times ...

I feel your strength.
I feel your power.
I feel your courage.
I feel your determination.
I feel your commitment.
I feel your fight.
I feel your love.

You are a Warrior.
You are a Blessed
You are Highly Favored.

YOU are my Hero.
YOU are my Inspiration.
YOU are my Beloved.

I love you.

From One Survivor to Another

I wrote this journal for women diagnosed with breast cancer that are truly ready to put on their big girl panties and boxing gloves to take the heavy weight belt. This journal is for CHAMPIONS! Fighting cancer is a knock-down-drag-out fight and in most cases, you don't get to train beforehand. You cannot go into this battle thinking pink and pretty "fight like a girl" thoughts. You must go in with the eye of a tiger… ready to fight for your life like a grown ass woman. It's literally kill or be killed. YOUR MIND has to be right! There's no time to feel sorry for yourself or for asking why me… it's in those moments of weakness that cancer will sucker punch you and take you down. This journal is designed to strengthen and empower as you go toe to toe with a notorious monster.

You will face your own fears and dig deep into your soul… On days when you don't feel like fighting, you will be reminded of what you are fighting for… when chemo has you down for the count and you feel like you can't get up, you will rise like a Phoenix!

When the pain is more than you can bare, you will find yourself taking the next punch and laughing as you prepare for a rope-a-dope.

It's important that you understand that this is not an easy fight and you will not win every round. You will get hit hard, knocked down, cut above the eye, hit in the back of the head, and cancer loves to hit below the belt… However, with the right attitude you will KNOCK OUT BREAST CANCER CHAMP! I did it, so can you! Gloves on. Let's go!

Subscribe to the **Fight Like a Grown Ass Woman Newsletter** for support, encouragement, and resources to help you through your journey. Sign up here: **www.Fight.LikeaGrownAssWoman.com**

"Your life is your story. Write well. Edit Often." ~Unknown

Write about the day you were diagnosed with cancer.

_____

_____

_____

_____

_____

_____

_____

_____

_____

_____

_____

_____

_____

_____

_____

_____

_____

_____

"Life has two rules. Number 1 never quit number 2 always remember rule number 1." ~Unknown

Write about why it's important to never give up.

_____
_____
_____
_____
_____
_____
_____
_____
_____
_____
_____
_____
_____
_____
_____
_____
_____
_____
_____
_____
_____
_____

"Be careful for nothing; but in everything by prayer and supplication with thanksgiving let your requests be made known to God." ~Philippians 4:6

Write about what you ask God for in prayer, supplication and with thanksgiving.

_____
_____
_____
_____
_____
_____
_____
_____
_____
_____
_____
_____
_____
_____
_____
_____
_____
_____
_____
_____
_____

"One comes to believe whatever one repeats to oneself sufficiently often, whether the statement be true or false. It comes to be dominating thought in one's mind." ~Robert Collier

Write affirmations and commit to saying them out loud

to yourself in a mirror every day.

"Team Work Makes The Dream Work!" ~Unknown

Write about your team ... the people who support you
and how they support you.

_____
_____
_____
_____
_____
_____
_____
_____
_____
_____
_____
_____
_____
_____
_____
_____
_____
_____
_____

"You cannot do a kindness too soon, for you never know how soon it will be too late."
~Ralph Waldo Emerson

Write about a kindness you will do for someone special in the next 5 days.

"Confess your faults one to another, and pray one for another, that you may be healed. The effectual fervent prayer of a righteous man avails much." ~James 5:16

Write about who you confess your faults to and who you pray for.

"Don't go into something to test the waters, go into things to make waves." ~Unknown Author

Write about how you can start making waves in life now.

"All I have seen teaches me to trust the Creator for all I have not seen." ~Ralph Waldo Emerson

Write about what you've seen that enables you to TRUST your Creator for what you have not seen but hope for.

_____
_____
_____
_____
_____
_____
_____
_____
_____
_____
_____
_____
_____
_____
_____
_____
_____
_____
_____
_____
_____
_____
_____

"Life is built of the things we do. The only constructive material is positive action." ~Unknown

Write about the positive action(s) that you are taking to build your life.

"Use what talent you possess. The woods would be very silent if
no birds sang there except those that sang best." ~UNKNOWN

List your talents and write about how you are using them.

"Every day is a gift from God. There's no guarantee of tomorrow, so that tells me to see the good in this day to make the most of it." ~Joel Osteen

Write about the GOOD that happened today

and how you made the most of it.

_____
_____
_____
_____
_____
_____
_____
_____
_____
_____
_____
_____
_____
_____
_____
_____
_____
_____
_____
_____
_____

"It took me quite a long time to develop a voice, and now that I have it, I am not going to be silent."
~Madeleine Albright

Write about what you are not going to be silent about.

"Do not give up, the beginning is always the hardest." ~Joel Osteen

Write about why it's always hardest at the beginning and

why giving up isn't an option.

"Life has many ways of testing a person's will, either by having nothing happen at all or by having everything happen all at once." ~Paulo Coelho

Write about how your will has been or is being tested.

_____

_____

_____

_____

_____

_____

_____

_____

_____

_____

_____

_____

_____

_____

_____

_____

_____

_____

_____

_____

_____

_____

"If you are in my life I am inspired by you in some shape or form." ~Unknown

Write about someone who inspires you.

_____
_____
_____
_____
_____
_____
_____
_____
_____
_____
_____
_____
_____
_____
_____
_____
_____
_____
_____
_____
_____
_____

"Power is not given to you. You have to take it." ~Beyonce Knowles

Write about what you are doing now and can do
in upcoming months to take your power.

Note to self. Sometimes you need to do what you don't feel like doing...
Write about something that you need to do but don't feel like doing.

"Trust in the LORD with all your heart, and lean not on your own understanding; in all your ways acknowledge Him, and He shall direct your paths." Proverbs 3:5-6

Write about a time when you trusted the Lord with all of your heart.

_____
_____
_____
_____
_____
_____
_____
_____
_____
_____
_____
_____
_____
_____
_____
_____
_____
_____
_____
_____
_____
_____
_____
_____
_____

"Even one small drop can make a ripple in the water and one small decision can affect your life in the simplest way." ~Unknown

Write about the most difficult decision you've ever had to make.

_____

_____

_____

_____

_____

_____

_____

_____

_____

_____

_____

_____

_____

_____

_____

_____

_____

_____

_____

_____

"To persevere is always a reflection of the state of one's inner life,
one's philosophy, and one's perspective." ~David Guterson

Write about the state of your inner life, your philosophy, and/or perspective.

"The greatest natural resource in the World is the spirit that resides in every unstoppable person" ~Cynthia Kersey

Write about what makes you unstoppable.

"Good things happen every day all around you… it's up to you to notice them." ~Marenda Taylor

Write about something GOOD or funny that happened to you today.

"Then they cried to the LORD in their trouble, and he saved them from their distress. He sent out his word and healed them; he rescued them from the grave. Let them give thanks to the LORD for his unfailing love and his wonderful deeds for mankind." ~Psalm 107:19-21

Write about what being healed and rescued from the grave means to you.

"The influence of a good teacher can never be erased." ~Unknown

Write about a teacher or someone who taught you an important life lesson that has had a lasting impact.

_____

_____

_____

_____

_____

_____

_____

_____

_____

_____

_____

_____

_____

_____

_____

_____

_____

_____

_____

"Adversity doesn't build character it reveals it!" ~Unknown

Write about what adversity has revealed to you about your character.

"Your own words are the bricks and mortar of the dreams you want to realize. Your words are the greatest power you have. The words you choose and their use establish the life you experience." ~Sonia Choquette

Write about the dreams you want to realize and read them out loud every day as a part of your morning or evening routine.

_____
_____
_____
_____
_____
_____
_____
_____
_____
_____
_____
_____
_____
_____
_____
_____
_____
_____
_____
_____
_____
_____

"Your greatest test is when you are able to bless someone else
while you are going through your own storm." ~Regina Malabago

Write about how you are helping other's while going through your own storm.

_____

_____

_____

_____

_____

_____

_____

_____

_____

_____

_____

_____

_____

_____

_____

_____

_____

_____

_____

"The LORD sustains them on their sickbed and restores them from their bed of illness." ~Psalm 41:3

Write about being sustained and restored by the Lord.

"You Never Hesitate To Tackle the Most Difficult Problems." ~Unknown

Write about the most difficult problem that you've tackled.

_____

_____

_____

_____

_____

_____

_____

_____

_____

_____

_____

_____

_____

_____

_____

_____

_____

_____

_____

_____

"Happiness keeps you Sweet, Trials keep you Strong, Sorrows keep you Human, Failures keep you Humble, Success keeps you Glowing, But Only God Keeps You Going!" ~Unknown

Write about how God keeps you going... give examples.

"Look for something positive in each day, even if some days you have to look a little harder." ~Unknown

Write about something positive that happened today.

"Accept what is, let go of what was, and have faith in what will be." ~Sonia Ricotti

Write about something that you must accept and let go of.

"Lots of people want to ride with you in the limo, but what you want is someone who will take the bus with you when the limo breaks down." ~Oprah Winfrey

Write about your ride or die, someone that will ride with you no matter what.

It's bigger than me...
Write about what "It's bigger than me" means to you.

"No matter what you look like or think you look like you're special and loved
and perfect just the way you are." ~Ariel Winter

Write about what makes you feel special and loved.

"Too positive to be Doubtful, Too Optimistic to be Fearful, and Too Determined to be Defeated." ~Unknown

Write about your strengths.

_____
_____
_____
_____
_____
_____
_____
_____
_____
_____
_____
_____
_____
_____
_____
_____
_____
_____
_____
_____
_____
_____

"A diamond is just a piece of charcoal that handled stress exceptionally well." ~Unknown

Write about how you handle stress.

"He gives strength to the weary and increases the power of the weak." ~Isaiah 40:29

Write about what or who gives you strength in times of weakness.

"Don't be the girl who fell. Be the girl who got back up." ~Jenette Stanley

Write about a time when you fell and got back up.

"I don't know what the future may hold, but I know who holds the future." ~Ralph Abernathy

Write about how you see your future.

"Love and appreciate your parents (and grandparents). We are often so busy growing up;
we forget they are also growing old." ~Unknown

Write about how you feel about watching your parents

(and grandparents) grow older.

_____

_____

_____

_____

_____

_____

_____

_____

_____

_____

_____

_____

_____

_____

_____

_____

_____

_____

_____

_____

"I know God will not give me anything I can't handle. I just wish that He didn't trust me so much."
~Mother Teresa

Write about what God trusts you with.

"Where There Is Love, There Is Life." ~Unknown

Write about Love and Life.

The Night before Chemo...

Write about your thoughts and feelings
the night before your 1st chemotherapy treatment.

_____
_____
_____
_____
_____
_____
_____
_____
_____
_____
_____
_____
_____
_____
_____
_____
_____
_____
_____
_____
_____

"The pain you feel today is the strength you feel tomorrow. For every challenge encountered there is opportunity for growth." ~Unknown

Write about the worse pain you've ever felt.

_____
_____
_____
_____
_____
_____
_____
_____
_____
_____
_____
_____
_____
_____
_____
_____
_____
_____
_____
_____

"Do you not know that your bodies are temples of the Holy Spirit, who is in you, whom you have received from God? You are not your own; you were bought at a price. Therefore honor God with your bodies."
~ 1 Corinthians 6.19-20

Write about how you honor God with your body.

"…did you know the people that are the strongest are usually the most sensitive? Did you know the people who exhibit the most kindness are the first to g et mistreated? Did you know the ones who take care of others all the time are usually the ones who ...

Write about saying I love you to someone you need to say it to
but haven't and write about asking for help.

"A woman is the full circle. Within her is the power to create, nurture and transform." ~Diane Mariechild

Write about who and or what you are creating, nurturing, and transforming.

"Laughter is good medicine." ~Proverbs 17:22

Write about something or someone who makes you laugh.

"Do one thing every day that scares you." ~Eleanor Roosevelt

Write about something that scares you.

_____

_____

_____

_____

_____

_____

_____

_____

_____

_____

_____

_____

_____

_____

_____

_____

_____

_____

_____

_____

_____

"I am not my hair, I am not this skin, I am a soul that lives within." ~India Arie

Write about what your experience with your hair has been since your 1st chemotherapy treatment and how you feel about it.

"Tough times never last, but tough people do." ~Dr. Robert Schuller

Write about what it means to be tough and if you consider yourself tough.

_____
_____
_____
_____
_____
_____
_____
_____
_____
_____
_____
_____
_____
_____
_____
_____
_____
_____
_____
_____

"Being challenged in life is inevitable, being defeated is optional." ~Roger Crawford

Write about the most difficult challenge you've ever faced.

"Women are never stronger than when they arm themselves with their weaknesses."
~Madame Marie du Deffand

Write about turning your weaknesses into strengths.

"Life shrinks or expands in proportion to one's courage." ~Anais Nin

Write about what courage means to you.

"Do your little bit of good where you are; it's those little bits of good put together that overwhelm the world."
~Desmond Tutu

Write about the little bits of good you did today to overwhelm the world.

"Remember, the greatest gift is not found in a store nor under a tree, but in the hearts of true friends."
~Cindy Lew

Write about your TRUE friends and how they are gifts to you.

"Nothing is so strong as gentleness, nothing so gentle as real strength." ~Saint Francis de Sales

Write about someone in your life who exemplifies real strength.

_____
_____
_____
_____
_____
_____
_____
_____
_____
_____
_____
_____
_____
_____
_____
_____
_____
_____
_____
_____
_____
_____
_____

"There are big ships and small ships. But the best ship of all is friendship." -Unknown
Write about how your friends responded to your diagnosis.

"If you even dream of beating me you'd better wake up and apologize." ~Muhammad Ali

Write things you would say to Cancer.

Love Abounds...
Write a poem about Love.

_____
_____
_____
_____
_____
_____
_____
_____
_____
_____
_____
_____
_____
_____
_____
_____
_____
_____
_____

"If you don't think every day is a good day, just try missing one." ~Cavett Robert

Write about what you would miss if you missed a day.

_____
_____
_____
_____
_____
_____
_____
_____
_____
_____
_____
_____
_____
_____
_____
_____
_____
_____
_____
_____

"Never surrender, it's all about the FAITH you got. don't ever stop, just push it 'til you hit the top and if you drop, at least you know you gave your all to be true to you, that way you can never fall." ~Tupac Shakur

Write about what it means to you "to be true to you."

"With everything that has happened to you, you can either feel sorry for yourself or treat what has happened as a gift. Everything is either an opportunity to grow or
an obstacle to keep you from growing. You get to choose." ~Wayne Dyer

Write about how you've grown since your diagnosis and treatment

"A lot of people are afraid to say what they want. That's why they don't get what they want." ~Madonna

Write about what you want then read it out loud.

_____
_____
_____
_____
_____
_____
_____
_____
_____
_____
_____
_____
_____
_____
_____
_____
_____
_____
_____
_____

"We all take different paths in life, but no matter where we go, we take a little of each other everywhere."
~Tim McGraw

Write about how you take others with you everywhere you go.

All the things that you're going through are building your character. You are being shaped and designed for your greatness. You have something special. You have GREATNESS within you!" ~Les Brown

Write about how you are taking the lemons

that life has thrown at you to make lemonade.

"I think if I've learned anything about friendship, it's to hang in, stay connected, fight for them, and let them fight for you. Don't walk away, don't be distracted, don't be too busy or tired, don't take them for granted. Friends are part of the glue that holds life and faith together. Powerful stuff." ~Jon Katz

Write about what you've learned about friends.

_____
_____
_____
_____
_____
_____
_____
_____
_____
_____
_____
_____
_____
_____
_____
_____
_____
_____
_____
_____

"When you have exhausted all possibilities, remember this. you haven't." ~Thomas Edison

Write about what the word POSSIBILITIES means to you.

_____

_____

_____

_____

_____

_____

_____

_____

_____

_____

_____

_____

_____

_____

_____

_____

_____

_____

_____

_____

"And once the storm is over, you won't remember how you made it through, how you managed to survive. You won't even be sure whether the storm is really over. But one thing is certain. When you come out of the storm, you won't be the same person who walked in. That's what this storm's all about."
~Haruki Murakami

Write about how you've changed.

"Determination burns within each one of us. Whether or not it will heat the room or the whole house depends on how much time we spend feeding the fire." ~Michelle C. Ustaszeski

Write about what you are determined to do.

"Having a rough morning? Place your hand over your heart...feel that? That's called purpose.
You're alive for a reason; Don't give up." ~Unknown

Write about your purpose.

"Your past doesn't define who you are. It just gives you the starting point for who you're going to be." ~Unkown

Write about who you are.

"It's our faith that activates the power of God." ~Joel Osteen

Write about the impact of your diagnosis and treatment on your faith and relationship with God.

_____

_____

_____

_____

_____

_____

_____

_____

_____

_____

_____

_____

_____

_____

_____

_____

_____

_____

_____

_____

_____

"The ocean stirs the heart, inspires the imagination and brings eternal joy to the soul."~Wyland
Write about what brings joy to your soul.

"We recognize a soulmate by the supreme level of comfort and security we feel with that person. That doesn't mean that there aren't issues that remain to be ironed out. Rather, it means we know intuitively that we can resolve issues with our soul mate without losing his or her love and respect." ~Linda Brady

Write about your soulmate.

"The love of a family is life's greatest blessings." ~Unknown

Write about who you consider your family to be
and how they are your greatest blessing.

"Mirror, Mirror on the wall..."
Write about how you see yourself and how you feel when you look in the mirror.

"Ways to create a better life. STOP -Playing the victim card -Making excuses -Letting society tell you how to live -Relying on others to make you happy -Doubting Yourself START -Enjoying alone time -Turning off gadgets and go outside -Positive thinking -Believing in yourself -Making your own happiness -Expressing your creativity -Acknowledging your desires/dreams/wishes -Make everything you want happen -Making your own happiness tips -Helping others realize they can make their own happiness" ~Unknown

Write about what you are doing to create a better life.

"Sail beyond the horizon; fly higher than you ever thought possible; magnify your existence by helping others; be kind to people and animals of all shapes and sizes; be true to what you value most; shine your light on the world; and be the person you were born to be." ~Blake Beattie

Write about how you do and will continue to shine your light on the world.

_____
_____
_____
_____
_____
_____
_____
_____
_____
_____
_____
_____
_____
_____
_____
_____
_____
_____
_____
_____
_____
_____

"We are as one with our ancestors and children."
~Rosita Worl Tlingit

Write about your concerns about your medical history of cancer
and how it affects your family.

"Twenty years from now you will be more disappointed by the things that you didn't do than by the ones you did do. So throw off the bowlines. Sail away from the safe harbor.
Catch the trade winds in your sails. Explore. Dream. Discover." ~Mark Twain

Write a list of things you've always wanted to do but haven't done yet.

"There is no medicine like hope, no incentive so great, and no tonic so powerful as expectation of something tomorrow." ~Orison Swett Marden

Write about your hopes, dreams, and expectations.

"Getting over a painful experience is much like crossing monkey bars.
You have to let go at some point in order to move forward." ~C.S. Lewis

Write about how you cope with painful experiences.

"One day your life will flash before your eyes. Make sure it's worth watching." ~Unknown
Write about a time when your life flashed before your eyes
and how it made you feel.

"It is impossible to feel grateful and depressed in the same moment." ~ Naomi Williams

Write about what you are grateful for.

"Good morning is not just a word, it's an action and a belief to live the entire day well. Morning is the time when you set the tone for the rest of the day. Set it right!" ~Fain Blake

Write about your morning routine and how you set the tone for each day.

It is only when we truly know and understand that we have a limited time on Earth and that we have no way of knowing when our time is up that we will begin to live each day to the fullest, as if it were the only one we had. ~Elisabeth Kubler-Ross.

Write about what you are doing to live each day to the fullest.

"Research has shown that support groups help reduce the three most significant stressors associated with cancer. unwanted aloneness, loss of control, and loss of hope." ~Cancer Support Community

Write about how you deal with the 3 most significant stressors associated with cancer and connecting with other survivors in a support group.

_____

_____

_____

_____

_____

_____

_____

_____

_____

_____

_____

_____

_____

_____

_____

_____

_____

_____

_____

_____

_____

_____

"The most important journey you will take in your life will usually be the one of self-transformation. Often, this is the scariest because it requires the greatest changes, in your life." ~Shannon L. Alder

Write about your self-transformation.

ABOUT THE AUTHOR

Marenda Taylor is a motivational speaker, writer and creator of the "Fight Like a Grown Ass Woman" movement and adult coloring book series. She is also the founder of "Know Her Body," a campaign to increase awareness among couples of the importance of frequent self-breast exams with a second pair of hands; inspired by Marenda's husband discovering a lump in her breast.

Marenda was diagnosed with triple negative breast cancer BRCA1+ at the age of 39 while working as a Senior Field Representative for a prominent elected official of the California State Legislature. Through chemotherapy, bilateral mastectomy, reconstructive surgeries and recovery, she made the conscious decision to take an integrative medicine approach addressing mind, body, and soul.

Marenda immersed herself in various therapies including Reiki, Mindfulness Meditation, Yoga, and fell in love with Writing for Wellness at the Cancer Support Community Redondo Beach. Her quest for healing and recovery ultimately led to Marenda leaving her "good government job" to pursue inspirational coaching, voice-over acting, photography, traveling and ultimately becoming a flight attendant.

Marenda has been featured on television programs and advertising campaigns that support breast cancer awareness and that include CBS Los Angeles News, Skin Wars, BCRF, a Haus of Volta Survivor Pinup Model and a Brand Ambassador for AnaOno Intimates. She has also served as a keynote speaker at breast cancer awareness and breast cancer support events around the country.

Marenda is dedicated to using her journey to encourage, educate, and empower women to Never Give Up and Fight Like A Grown Ass Woman … no matter what.

"Ladies, when life throws you lemons, put on your boxing gloves, make pink lemonade and fight like a grown ass woman!"
~Marenda

Yoga Like a Grown Ass Woman

VOLUME 1 COLORING BOOK

A Meditative Coloring Journey of Grace, Purpose, and Passion for Evolving Women

BY MARENDA TAYLOR

Made in the USA
Monee, IL
08 July 2020